A St Ives Tru t

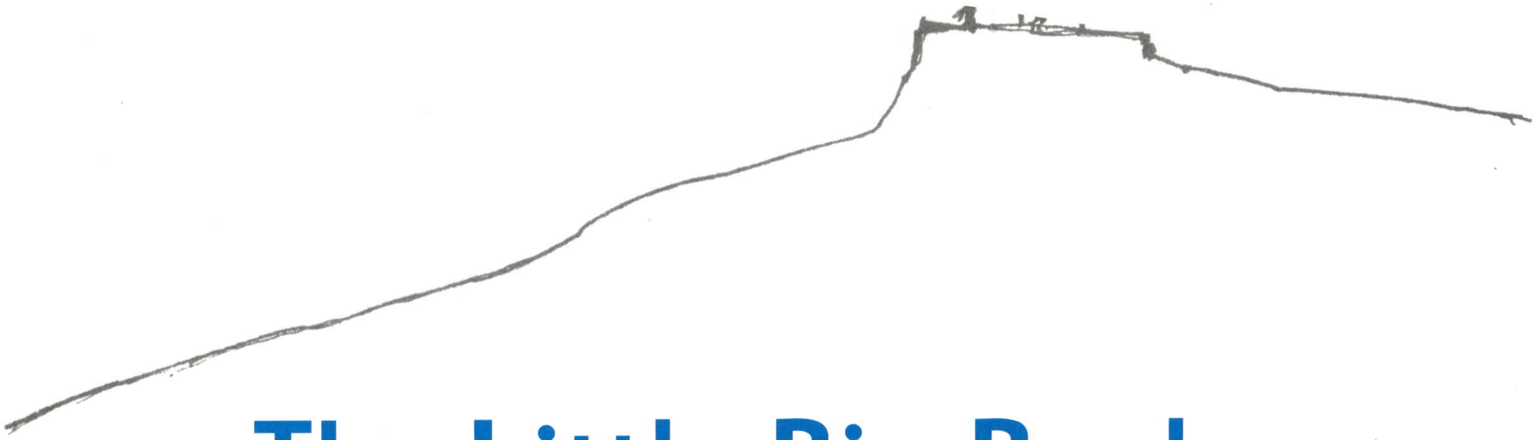

The Little Big Book of Seaside Holidays

By Mary Quick

Illustrated by Steve Martin

Supported by

First Great Western

The title of this book derives from the limited edition publication
The Big Book of Seaside Holidays
produced in 2006 by St Ives Trust Archive Study Centre
supported by MLA South West with funding from DCMS and DfES,
Penwith District Council and the Royal Cornwall Museum

The limited edition was so popular that the Archive Study Centre was
asked to produce a smaller children's picture book version
hence *The Little Big Book of Seaside Holidays*

This publication first published in 2006
by St Ives Trust
Upper Parish Room, St Andrew's Street
St Ives, Cornwall, TR26 1AH, UK
Tel: 01736 796408
Website: www.stivestrust.co.uk
E-mail: archive@stivestrust.co.uk
Charity number 254692

ISBN No. 0-9554398-0-9

Printed by Eden Print Limited, Redruth, TR16 4AX. Tel: 01209 202190.

The Little Big Book of Seaside Holidays

By Mary Quick

Illustrated by Steve Martin

Our story starts long ago when Christine and Ken came to the seaside on holiday. They brought their children, Katherine and Mark. Mark looked out of the train window. He saw the sea first and shouted, 'I can see it, I can see it!'

They always stayed with Mrs. Clark and her father Bob, who used to be a fisherman. He lived with her. Christine went to the shops to buy the food and Mrs. Clark cooked the family's meals. Sometimes she made delicious Cornish pasties. For tea, she made another treat, scones with jam and cream on top.

GWR
4517
GWR

Old Bob said they could call him 'Granda Bob'. Sometimes he took Katherine and Mark for rides around the Bay in his rowing boat, the Lily. One day, Granda Bob broke an oar in his boat. He came home with the broken oar in one hand. On the fingers of his other hand he carried some fresh mackerel he had caught. All the next day he was busy in his cellar making a special surprise for Katherine.

Next day, he showed her a painted wooden doll. 'This doll is called Joanie,' he said, 'I made her for you out of that old oar.' He whispered, 'Joanies are special. They look after everyone who paddles, or swims in the sea, or goes for boat rides. They can do magic!' He gave Katherine the doll.

Katherine was delighted. She thanked him and showed Joanie to Mum and Dad. After that, Joanie went everywhere with her. Katherine and Mark played bat-and-ball on the beach with other children. They built sand-castles and looked for tiny crabs under the seaweed. They climbed the rocks and fished in the rock pools.

The fishermen caught all kinds of fish. The fish were spread out on the slipway to be sold. The fish were brought in from the boats by horse and cart. The driver's small dog ran along under the cart. Katherine was afraid the little dog would be run over. But Joanie knew he would be all right. Big ships tied up by the pier.

They brought coal for the gas works.

There were French boats that fished for crabs. The French fishermen wore colourful red or blue suits. They paid for their shopping with crabs. Artists set up their easels. The people who passed by stopped to look at their paintings.

When they walked on the headland, Katherine and Mark saw fishing nets spread out to dry. The nets had been dipped in a special brown liquid to stop them from rotting.

CM2467

Cats were everywhere, black and white, ginger and striped. Katherine and Mark had never seen so many cats. They were in the streets and sunning themselves on window ledges. Katherine stroked them and talked to them. They answered with loud purrs. She told them to be good and not climb in to steal food.

Not all the cats had homes. 'So where do these cats get their food, Dad? Who feeds them?' Dad explained that everyone fed them, especially the fishermen. The cats slept in buildings called lofts where all the fishing nets were kept. They stopped the mice from eating the nets.

Katherine said, 'I know a nursery rhyme about cats.' 'Bet you don't,' answered Mark. 'Oh, I do, I do!' 'Go on then, let's hear it.'

'As I was going to St. Ives, I met a man with 7 wives.
Each wife had 7 sacks, Each sack had 7 cats, Each cat had 7 kits,
Kits, cats, sacks, wives, how many were there going to St. Ives?'

'Don't know,' said Mark, 'How many?' 'Mustn't tell,' laughed Katherine. 'It's a secret!' But Joanie knew. Do you? Washing was hung on clothes lines tied from house to house in the narrow old-fashioned streets.

Every year, the Sunday Schools had a special Tea-Treat. They marched around the town holding their banners. In front was the Salvation Army band. On the headland, the grown-ups had tea and the children drank fizzy pop and ate huge saffron buns. Katherine and Mark found it hard to eat all of their buns. Afterwards everybody played games.

Regatta Day was exciting. There were swimming races. Boys tried to climb a slippery pole. Sailing boats raced out in the Bay. In the evening there was a Carnival led by the Town Band. The Carnival Queen and her attendants wore pretty dresses. Katherine cuddled Joanie, who wished she could tap her wooden feet to the music. Mum said they could take a present home. Katherine looked in all the little shops. She chose a big shell. Joanie had to say 'Goodbye' to Katherine. Granda Bob thought Joanie wouldn't like living in a big city. He would look after Joanie until they came back.

When Katherine was grown up she brought her own family back to her favourite seaside town for their holidays. She came with her husband Phil, and their daughter Rose. When they rode in the little train, Katherine remembered the steam engine. The diesel train was not so exciting. They stayed at Pam's Bed and Breakfast. Mrs. Clark was Pam's aunty. Mrs. Clark came to see them and she brought Joanie. Katherine was excited to see Joanie again, and she gave her to Rose to look after.

Katherine noticed the seaside had changed since she was a little girl. Now visitors went for rides in motor boats instead of little rowing boats. The family sailed along the coast in the Cornish Belle. They saw seals on the rocks in the sun. One day they went on a fishing trip and caught some mackerel. They took the fish home and Pam cooked them for tea.

Mum and Dad rented a tent on the beach and Rose made friends with children she met there. In little pools hidden in the rocks, the children caught tiny shrimps with fishing nets. They played cricket, rounders and football. They made sand-castles and splashed each other in the sea. Rose was in and out of the water all day long.

TIMES & ECHO

When she was not in the sea, Rose enjoyed Hart's famous ice-cream at the harbour. On the harbour wall sat beatniks with beards and long hair and ragged jeans. The beatniks played guitars.

On the beach, Uncle Harold held children's meetings called sand-services. They were like Sunday School, with talks and singing. Rose liked the sand-services. So did Joanie.

On wet afternoons they went to the cinema and watched Disney films. Rose loved them. So did Mum and Dad. Sometimes on fine evenings, there were water-polo matches in the harbour. The swimmers tried to score a goal by throwing the ball into the net.

St.Ives
Hayle
PARIS

After the boats sailed in their Regatta, there was a Carnival in the evening. Rose thought it was wonderful. A lorry decorated with flowers carried the Carnival Queen and her attendants. Following behind were more lorries. There was Mickey Mouse and his friends, and fishermen with their nets full of fish made of silver paper. People in fancy dress would join in and follow the lorries.

SS116
BOOK HERE for THE
CORNISHBELLE

One morning, they were having breakfast when BANG! BANG! Two rockets went off in the sky. Rose jumped. Mum explained that the rockets were to call out the lifeboat. Mum told Rose that when she was a little girl, hundreds of men pulled the lifeboat into the sea with long ropes. Rose and her Mum went down to the harbour. Crowds gathered to watch a tractor tow the lifeboat down to the sea. The boat went into the water with a splash and raced off to the rescue.

On Lifeboat Day the lifeboat went on show, dressed with flags. It took people for rides around the Bay. Rose went for a thrilling trip in the lifeboat with Mum and Dad. Afterwards they gave money to the Lifeboat Fund.

Often, bands played on the band-stand in the harbour. On Sunday evenings, the Salvation Army marched to the beat beat beat of their drums, waving their banners. They held a service on the slipway. Rose, and Mum and Dad liked to sing along with the crowd. Joanie hummed the tunes.

All too soon the holiday was over. Mum said it was time to go home. But they knew they would come again. Joanie stayed at the seaside with Pam. But she knew her magic would bring the family back again.

THE SLOOP INN

The family still comes to the seaside. Now Rose is grown up and she has her own family. Her husband Eric drove her and twins Louise and John in their car. So Katherine is a Granny. Sometimes Granny Katherine comes on holiday with them, but she finds the seaside has changed a lot since she was a little girl. There are long traffic jams of cars. They stay in a cottage near the beach. Long ago, fishermen and their families lived in the cottage, now people on holiday stay there. Pam came to see them and guess who she brought with her? That's right, Joanie. On fine evenings the family have barbecues on the sand, and watch crowds of surfers ride the waves. Now the beach is crowded all day long, lifeguards make sure everyone is safe. Joanie is pleased about this.

The narrow streets are full of holiday-makers. The sea is noisy with self-drive motor boats. All around the harbour, boatmen call to the holiday-makers, 'Boat trips leaving soon. See the seals and catch a mackerel.' The little shops that Granny Katherine remembered are now restaurants and take-aways. There are lots of galleries that sell paintings.

Tate Gallery
t. Ives Museum
RAC
CORNWALL
GUIDE
TRAFFIC WARD
StIves

There are still the Sunday School Treats that Granny remembers. The twins march with other children and enjoy their buns and fizzy drink, and the games afterwards. Joanie wasn't so pleased, as Louise left her behind and took Barbie instead.

One evening they watched the raft races in the harbour. The rafts are made from old plastic barrels and anything that will float. The young people on the rafts try to tip each other over. They throw bags of flour. It is all good fun. Louise and John enjoy it. So do the crowds watching around the harbour.

People eat Cornish pasties, fish and chips and ice-creams in the streets and around the harbour. Some have a nasty shock when seagulls swoop down and steal the food from their fingers.

START
ANNUAL RAFT RACE

Sometimes the family go to the children's theatre, Kidz R Us. Granny remembers when the theatre was the Wesley Chapel. The children sing and dance and act. They are very good.

One day the Radio One Roadshow came to the football field. Hundreds of people went to hear the music and see their favourite pop stars.

When the stars appeared, everyone screamed and shouted. Louise and John, with Mum and Dad went to the Roadshow.

RADIO ONE
ROADSHOW
BBC

Granny stayed at home and Joanie was glad of her company. Granny loves the seaside, but she misses things from when she was a little girl. Granny misses the Regatta, the Carnivals, the bands playing and artists painting their pictures. Granny misses Mrs. Clark and Granda Bob, who carved Joanie from the broken oar. But where is Joanie?

Joanie is sad. Louise seems to like Barbie best. One day when they went to the Museum, Joanie used her magic to hide away. Soon a woodcarver found Joanie. He thought she was very special. He decided to copy her and make some more Joanies. So now Joanie has some friends to keep her company. When visitors come to the Museum, they always want to see them. That makes Joanie very proud!

ST. IVES
MUSEUM

A note about the Great Western Railway and Seaside Holidays

Children playing on the sands 1938. *Copyright David Elsbury.*

Isambard Kingdom Brunel's *Royal Albert Bridge* over the River Tamar at Saltash was opened on May 2nd 1859, providing Cornwall with a through railway link with the rest of the country, attracting visitors and artists to the far west.

The Great Western Railway soon gained a reputation for speed, reliability and service which earned it the affectionate title of 'God's Wonderful Railway'. Its locomotives, painted in 'Great Western green' and the chocolate-and-cream livery of the passenger coaches soon became famous.

Branch lines were established to many seaside towns and villages which before long blossomed as holidays resorts. The St Ives branch line from St Erth (formerly St Ives Road) station, opened in 1877, was the last section of broad gauge railway to be built. In 1892 the whole of the Great Western Railway system was converted from the broad gauge (7ft.0¼in) to standard gauge (4ft. 8½ins) over one weekend in May 1892.

The G.W.R. invented the name 'Carbis Bay' for the station on the St Ives branch line serving the hamlet which subsequently flourished with granite villas, hotels and guesthouses.

The early visitors were often well-off people, important enough to be listed in the local newspaper. Holidays for ordinary people began with the families of railway workers from Swindon who had free rail travel to their chosen destination, many of them choosing St Ives. They often returned year after year to the same landladies. 'Swindon Week' in early July was a lively time for the Cornish holiday resorts.

Fortunately the St Ives branch line was reprieved from the Beeching axe of 1963, but its fine Victorian granite station building was demolished in 1969.

The Great Western Railway was active in promoting holiday travel with posters, booklets and 'Holiday Haunts', annual lists of hotels and accommodation at resorts served by the system.

Steam train on the St Ives branch line c.1960.